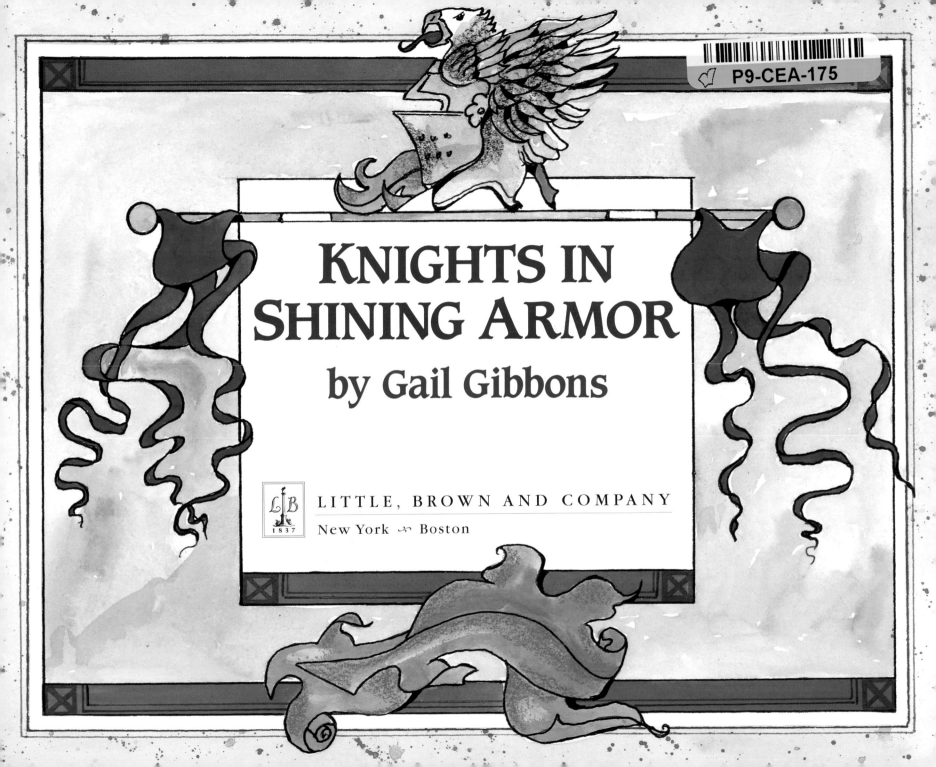

KNIGHTS IN SHINING ARMOR

by Gail Gibbons

LITTLE, BROWN AND COMPANY

New York ❧ Boston

Little, Brown and Company

Hachette Book Group USA
237 Park Avenue, New York, NY 10017
Visit our Web site at www.lb-kids.com

First Paperback Edition: April 1998

Library of Congress Cataloging-in-Publication Data

Gibbons, Gail
    Knights in shining armor / by Gail Gibbons.—1st ed.
       p.   cm.
    ISBN 978-0-316-30948-6 (hc) ISBN 978-0-316-30038-4 (pb)
    1. Knights and knighthood — History — Juvenile literature.
2. Chivalry — History — Juvenile literature.   3. Armor — History —
Juvenile literature.   [1. Knights and knighthood.]   I. Title.
CR4513.G48   1995
394'.7 — dc20   94-35525

                    10   9   8   7   6   5 (hc)
                    15   14   13   12 (pb)

                              SC

                    Manufactured in China

The illustrations for this book were done in watercolors, colored pencil, and black
pen on 140-weight D'Arches watercolor paper.

The period known as the Middle Ages, from 500 to 1500 A.D., was also the Age of Knights.

Knights were the best fighters in Europe during that time. They wore strong armor and fought on horseback with deadly weapons. Their entire way of life was based on warfare.

Called *ritters* in Germany, *chevaliers* in France, and *caballeros* in Spain, these fearless warriors pledged their loyalty to their kings, queens, or lords. They agreed to fight their rulers' enemies whenever called upon. In exchange, they were given large plots of land and the right to rule over the peasants who lived and worked on them. This method of government is called the feudal system.

The most powerful knights ruled over the nearby countryside from huge stone castles. Surrounded by high walls and deep moats filled with water, these castles were fortresses that provided refuge and protection during times of war.

STABLES

TOWER

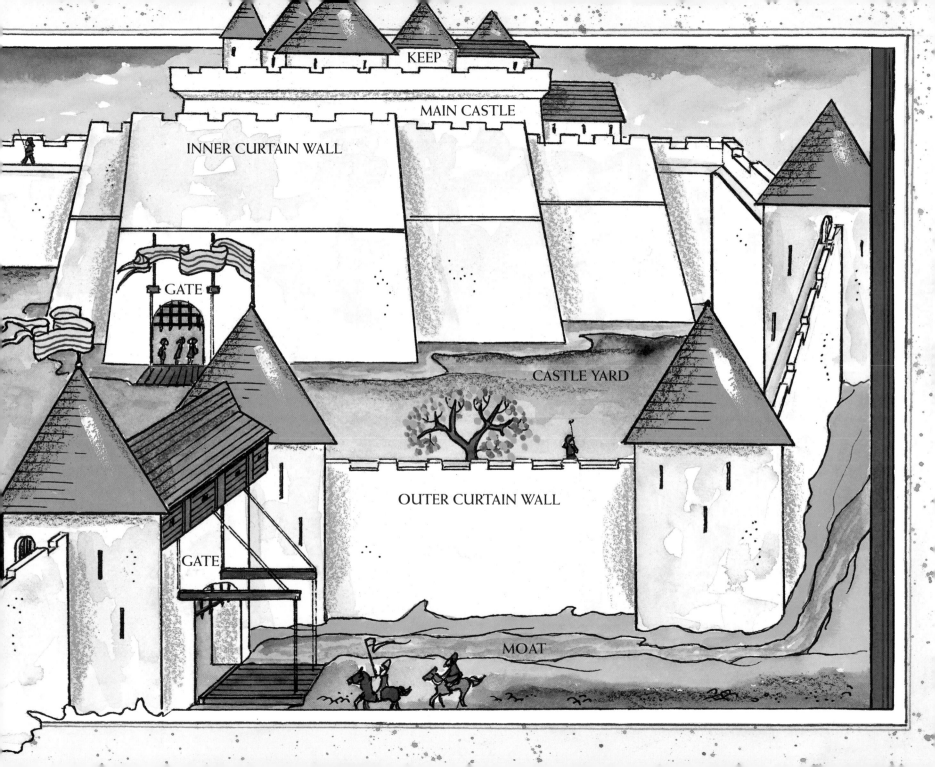

KEEP

MAIN CASTLE

INNER CURTAIN WALL

GATE

CASTLE YARD

GATE

OUTER CURTAIN WALL

MOAT

It took many years of training to become a knight. First, at age seven, a boy became a page. Until his teens, he served his master, who was already a knight, as well as his master's family. From his master, the page learned how to fight with swords and to hunt using falcons and hawks. To improve his abilities, he played games of skill and strategy.

PAGE

SQUIRE

Next the page became a squire. A squire practiced handling weapons and became a skilled horseman. The squire continued to serve his master and also rode by his side in battle.

After years of training and practice, the squire was ready to become a knight. Any knight could grant knighthood to a squire by saying "I dub thee knight" at a special ceremony. Some squires were knighted on the battlefield as recognition for great bravery during a fight. The new knight was given his weapons and sword by his master or ruler. Now the title *Sir* was placed in front of his name.

KNIGHT

SHIELD

To protect himself in battle, a knight carried a light wooden shield. Usually covered in leather and edged in metal, the shield was also decorated with the knight's emblem, or coat of arms. The emblem could be an eagle, a bear, a dragon, a lion, or anything he wanted. A knight became famous by showing his coat of arms on many battlefields.

COAT OF ARMS

LANCE

The knight's most important weapons were his lance and his sword. He used the lance on horseback. He pointed it at his opponent and rode toward him as fast as he could. The knight tried to kill his enemy, or knock him off his horse, with a single blow—before his enemy could do the same to him.

SWORD

If his lance broke or his enemy forced him off his horse, the knight had to fight with his sword. Knights clashed their swords together as they fought face-to-face on the battlefield.

BATTLE-AX

FLAIL

MACE

Knights also used other weapons. They fought with flails, spiked iron balls swung on chains, and war clubs called maces, which had heavy iron heads. Sometimes they used the deadly battle-ax.

HELMET

GARMENT

HAUBERK

Along with his weapons, a knight needed armor to protect his body during battle. In the early Middle Ages, this armor included a leather garment or a heavy cloth that covered most of the knight's body. On top of this, the knight wore a hauberk, a tunic made of linked iron rings called chain mail. The hauberk had a hood that protected the knight's head and neck. He also wore a steel helmet.

HELMET

VISOR

SHOULDER PLATE

BREASTPLATE

ELBOW CAP

GAUNTLET

CUISSE

SHIN GUARD

In the late Middle Ages, knights' armor was much heavier. It weighed about fifty-five pounds and was made of strong metal plates lined with soft material to protect the knight's skin. He also wore a helmet with a heavy visor that lowered to cover his face. The whole outfit was so heavy that sometimes a knight needed help mounting his horse.

A knight's horse was probably his most valuable possession. Success in battle depended as much on the strength, quickness, and bravery of his horse as it did on his own abilities. Knights gave their horses special names and considered them companions-in-arms.

Battles between knights were not as scary as one might think. Many of their battles were small, sometimes only a few hundred men, and often they lasted just a few hours. A knight would rather catch his enemy than kill him, because then he could hold him for ransom.

Many battles were fought over land and property disputes. To lose a battle could mean the loss of an army or the end of a king's or queen's rule. Some knights raided enemy territories for horses, supplies, or other treasures of the kingdom.

Legends from the past often mention knights fighting dragons. These mythical creatures were believed to be evil, monstrous serpents with wings and prickly scales. The legend of Saint George tells how he bravely slew a dragon to save a princess in distress. Stories like this one helped keep alive the knights' beliefs in dragons.

Sometimes the knights of a kingdom would perform fake battles called tournaments or tourneys. People in the Middle Ages attended these tourneys much as people today attend a football game or other sporting event. Gaily dressed crowds of royalty and peasants cheered on their favorite knights, as colorful banners fluttered over the field.

The knights tested each other's skills by fighting with blunted swords and flattened lances. They didn't want to hurt their opponents, but often, in an event so much like a battle, accidents and injuries occurred.

Most knights followed a code for good behavior. These good knights believed they should be generous to the poor, protect their faith and the church, and defend those who couldn't defend themselves. These rules were called the code of chivalry.

Knights followed similar rules of chivalry during battle, too. When one knight took another knight captive, he would treat him as an honored guest. And a chivalrous knight would never attack without warning. Such behavior was considered unworthy of a true knight.

Ladies had their own ideas of how a noble knight should act. They believed a chivalrous knight honored women, especially the one he loved and had sworn his devotion to. A knight would remain loyal to his lady and perform great deeds in her name.

But not all knights followed the code of chivalry. Some did just the opposite. They robbed and plundered for their own gain. A knight who was proved guilty of bad behavior or cowardice was disgraced by having his sword and spurs broken. Without his weapon and the means to control his horse, he was no longer a knight.

Today, knighthood doesn't have the same meaning it did during the Middle Ages. Modern knights are also honored when they have done a great deed that benefits others, but their lives are not necessarily based on warfare. Many scientists, artists, writers, military figures, and explorers have been given knighthood. Men add the title *Sir* before their names just as they did in the Middle Ages. Women honored in this way are given the title *Dame*.

Throughout history, tales and songs have been written and sung of famous knights and the brave acts they performed. The exciting stories of these legendary men, the most respected warriors of the Middle Ages, continue to be told today.

King Arthur and His Famous Knights

KING ARTHUR was the legendary sixth-century king who ruled England. His knights were called the Knights of the Round Table, because they supposedly met around a circular table, showing they were equal. King Arthur insisted his knights be brave, strong, loyal, humble, courteous, and devoted to the church.

SIR GAWAIN was wise and courteous. Squires and pages looked to him as an example of what a knight should be.

SIR GARETH was a brave knight and warrior. He fought many enemies and in turn won the hand of the Lady of Lyonesse.

SIR TRISTRAM was a very powerful knight in battle, even against enormous odds. One of his fiercest battles was against the determined knight Sir Marhaus. They fought for two long hours until Sir Tristram finally triumphed.

SIR LANCELOT was the most celebrated knight in all the world. He performed many deeds of great bravery.

SIR GALAHAD was the hero of the most famous quest in the legends of King Arthur and his knights. He found the Holy Grail, a cup that was believed to have been used by Christ at the Last Supper.

Dragon Legends

SAINT GEORGE was a noble savior who once rescued an entire village from an evil, hungry dragon.

FAFNIR was a fearsome legendary dragon who guarded a cave filled with a great treasure of gold. He was finally defeated by Siegfried, a famous knight.

SIR LANCELOT was known throughout all the lands as a dragon slayer. He killed dragons in battles that sometimes lasted for several days.